Multihulls

ALSO BY ROBIN G. COLES

Boating Secrets: 127 Top Tips to Help You Buy and/or Enjoy Your Boat

Buying a Boat, an Interview w/Captain Chris Kourtakis

Marine Surveys, an Interview w/Rob Scanlan

Insuring a Boat, an Interview w/Mike Smith

Financing a Boat Purchase, an Interview w/Jim Coburn

Rent Your Boat, an Interview w/Brian Stefka

Search and Rescue, an Interview w/Alan Sorum

Bad Storms/Heavy Weather, an Interview w/Timothy Wyand

Digital Selective Calling (DSC), the Automatic Identification System (AIS), and Automated Radio Checks (ARC), an Interview w/Captain Chris Kourtakis

Multihulls, an Interview w/Jim Brown

Custom Electrical Panels and Wiring Harnesses, an Interview w/Mark Rogers

Making a Living as a Professional Sailor, an Interview w/Brian Hancock

Seven Tips for a Successful Sale of Your Used Boat

4 Essential Steps to Buying Your Boat

Or, go to: Boating Secrets Website (BoatingSecrets127TopTips.com) for all our books, audios, and transcripts

Multihulls

An Interview with Jim Brown

Robin G. Coles

TheNauticalLifestyle.com

Multihulls: An Interview with Jim Brown

www.TheNauticalLifestyle.com
ISBN: 0983638152
ISBN-13:   978-0-983681-5-5

Dedication

For my aunt, Ruth Shoer, who passed away before this book was finished.

I miss you!

"Why Haven't Boat Owners Been Told These Facts Before?"

Karen G. Gales
TheYachtLady.com

You already know buying a boat is one of the most challenging things you'll ever do in your life. And, it's an awesome way to include both your family and friends. Not to mention all the fun you'll have out on the water. But, do you know the...

✓ Do's and don'ts when buying a boat

✓ Two little known tools surveyors use to determine a boat's age and condition

✓ Three surprising reasons why marinas require the insurance they do

✓ How you can still get a boat loan even if your credit score is less than 720

✓ How a commercial emergency signaling technology has saved more than 25,000 lives since 1982 and is now available for pleasure boaters

✓ What to do when you get caught in a bad storm or heavy weather

✓ Why customizing your electrical and instrument panels makes sense

✓ How Digital Selective Calling and the Automated Identification System saves lives in a Search and Rescue Operation

✓ The advantages and disadvantages of having a multihull craft over a monohull

✓ Three powerful strategies you can use to best prepare your boat for rentals

✓ What's changed to take sailing from an amateur sport to top of the game earning a decent living

Now imagine having eleven of the top marine industry experts sitting with you and spilling all of these secrets plus more. Well... now you can!

Introducing...

A complete guide for new and seasoned boaters to buy and enjoy your boat

Boating Secrets

117 Top Tips to Help You Buy and Enjoy Your Boat, Revealed by Eleven Marine Industry Experts
Vol. 1

Boating Secrets Testimonials

Robin Coles has impressed me very much as a friend and an advocate to the marine industry. Her website TheNauticalLifestyle.com has become a work of "internet art" for the average boater.

I listened to her discussions with industry experts that are the basis for her book and was totally impressed at the quality of her participating experts, their knowledge and Robin's ability to ask the right questions, as well as her follow up questions.

Anyone seeking to purchase a new boat or intending to buy a larger boat should have her book in their library.

Captain Leo Corsetti, Arlington, MA, Retired, Tone President,
Proud Tartan Owner

~~~

Robin Coles has done a wonderful job of covering a comprehensive list of topics that will help new and experienced boaters get the most out of their investment.

An educated boater is a better boater and a better boater is much more likely to enjoy a lifetime of fun with family and friends.

Robin taps into many of the recreational boating industry's most experienced experts who will help you avoid many of the situations that inexperienced boaters could find themselves in. A boat is a significant investment of your time in an era where free time is much harder to come by.

This Nautical Lifestyle Expert Series is sure to help you maximize your investment while making you a better captain when you inevitably find yourselves in harrowing situations. As the captain, you take on huge responsibilities and it's important that boating safety is always top of mind. It may save your life or one of your loved ones.

Carl Blackwell, Vice President, Discover Boating,
National Marine Manufacturers Association (NMMA)

Table of Contents

Author's Introduction

So why am I writing or, more to the point, why did I make this interview series into a book?

Not everyone likes to listen or learns by listening. Some of us still like holding a book in our hands, feeling the weight of it on our laps, and even going through it page by page with a highlighter and marking what's important to us as we read. I'm one of those rare birds who still likes to hold a book and feel its weight in the crook of my arm while I have a good cup of tea. Others nowadays are reading books on their computers or even on Amazon's Kindle or Barnes and Noble's NOOK. Who knows? There might even be something new by the time you read this. I also find that a reference book, which this certainly could be, is great when it's accessible on your book shelf—you can quickly thumb through it to find the information you're looking for. You could add a different colored sticky note to the first page of each chapter for quick reference.

Others learn by listening, and that's great too! But I wanted to make sure I had this book in different media for everybody. That's how important I believe this project is. It's important because for years now, as I've learned more and more about boating, I've found there isn't a lot of basic information out there; and the information that I can find is scattered all over the place. Also, I'm not always sure of the credentials of the people writing articles about boating.

But, let's back up a few years and start at the beginning.

Growing up, I always had a fascination for the ocean and the skies—the moon and the stars. At night I would watch the moon follow me around and search the sky for the big dipper, little dipper, Hercules, and other constellations. When I was a little girl, my aunt Dee would take me to Revere Beach and we would walk the beach. She never let me go into the water without shoes on my feet for fear of seaweed wrapping around my legs and pulling me under. (What wearing shoes had to do with that, I'm not sure.) So I never went into the water, but always dreamed about it. When I got my own car I would head to Storrow and Memorial Drives on my lunch breaks and watch the sailboats on the Charles River, wishing it was me on one of them. (I also had a fascination for airplanes—watching them take off and land at airports—but that's another story for another time. Maybe I've just wanted to escape from day-to-day life. I guess that's why I now live near both an airport and the ocean.)

Fast forward to April 5, 2001. I was told over the phone that I had cancer. A couple of days later, in the doctor's office, I was told that I had less than ten years to live. The year before I'd been misdiagnosed with multiple sclerosis and told that I'd be confined to a wheel chair within a year. Doctors can be so cruel in what they tell you and, more importantly, how they tell you. After I came to terms with this news, and after I grieved for the person I once knew and had been, I set out to make some changes in my life. It was time to conquer my fear of being on the ocean. I called a friend of mine and asked him to take me kayaking. He did, and that experience really changed my outlook. Kayaking was so peaceful and fun. If I hadn't almost been hit by a tanker, I probably would have gone again. Of course, I'd also been afraid of tipping over (I'm not a very good swimmer), an odd fear to have surfaced in me since my sons and I had done a lot of canoeing and rowing during our many camping trips when they were young and I hadn't been afraid then.

Next, I took up sailing. I had looked into sailing on the Charles River, but at that school one first had to pass a swim test, which I didn't believe I could do, and I really wanted to learn on the ocean. Ocean sailing was an experience that I found to be the epitome of relaxation. I absolutely fell in love with sailing and couldn't get out into Boston Harbor enough. Mark, my primary sailing instructor, had so much passion both for the sport and for teaching that he made learning to sail really enjoyable. As with everything, some of my instructors were better than others. But

Mark was awesome and whenever I went sailing on the 23-foot Sonar, I felt the boat and I were one. I could hop into the cockpit, grab the tiller, and feel her every move as we'd glide through the waves.

One day I went to the Sailing Center with a sailing buddy and we took out a boat with which neither of us was familiar. The boat was six feet longer than what we were used to and it had a steering wheel. I had never sailed a boat with a wheel before, but off we went. This was something new to learn—great! Wrong. Neither of us was experienced with this size or type of boat and we had no business taking it out by ourselves. What happened to us that afternoon would never have happened if we had taken out the 23-foot Sonar instead. We got caught in a couple of wind and rain storms. We tried taking the sails down, but the furlings came off. The wind kept pushing us sideways. I was trying to hold the wheel and watch the skipper on deck to make sure he didn't fall overboard. The wind and rain squall picked up and pushed us right onto the beach—we ended up going aground. Then the engine wouldn't start and we had to call Sea Tow. One of the topics we discuss in this book is heavy weather. A big part of that is knowing your boat, which neither of us did. It was scary.

In 2006, I went to a National Geographic Travel Writing workshop in New York. There I met a woman who also loved sailing and we hung out together for the day. When the workshop was over, she told me that she knew someone who was looking for a reviewer, writer, and photographer for a cruising guide book. She suggested I take a look at the website and then call her if I was interested. I did. A few days later, the publisher called me. That year, after they'd trained me, the project was cancelled. In 2007, the project was on again, so off I went.

My assignment was to review, write about, and photograph over 200 marinas from Block Island, Rhode Island, to St. John's River in New Brunswick, Canada. I spent three months on the road, staying in hotels, motels, and bed and breakfasts, keeping a ridiculous schedule in order to get that project done. One thing I learned along the way is that boaters are a very friendly group. There's a different mindset when you're on the water versus being in the corporate grind every day. I liked it. For a number of other reasons, this project turned sour and never came to fruition.

But it was during this project that I met Chuck, the local harbormaster, and got to know and work alongside him. It was also during this time that Winthrop, Massachusetts, the town I'd just moved back to, was putting in a new marina. There were lots of questions being asked, and speculations being made, by the townspeople about the new marina. I approached Chuck the following spring and we did an interview which I recorded and put up on the web. This interview answered a lot of questions for the residents and the project continued with fewer objections. For a while after that I wrote a weekly column for the local newspaper reporting on activities at the local marinas and yacht clubs.

Around that time I started studying marketing on the internet with Mark Hendricks. I needed something to work on and decided to take everything I'd learned during the project from hell and turn it into something positive. This new project became TheNauticalLifestyle.com and it is always evolving. I'm not afraid to try something new and if it sticks, great. If not, why not?

One thing I learned during both projects is that I love interviewing people—I guess it goes with that curious mind of mine. You know how some children are always asking why, why, why? That's me, still to this day—always asking why; always seeking, searching for answers. But it can't be just any answer—it has to make sense.

Content, content, content is what Google looks for and what Mark stresses in his internet marketing lessons. So I posted a request on LinkedIn indicating that I was looking for speakers for an interview series that I was putting together. The rest, as they say, is history.

In this book I have tried to cover all of the basics as well as some more advanced boating topics for the old salts. It's filled with lots of answers that should enhance your boating experiences. Interviewing these knowledgeable gentlemen has taught me a lot and it's truly been a pleasure working with them. My wish is for you to get just as much out of reading this book as I have in putting it together.

The final reason for creating this book is that as I have ventured out on my journey to become a better boater, I've had many questions. What better way to get them answered than to interview the experts? So that's what I did.

Multihulls
An Interview with Jim Brown

Introduction

Robin: Hello everyone. This is Robin Coles and it's my pleasure to welcome you to the Nautical Lifestyle Expert Series brought to you by TheNauticalLifestyle.com. During the next hour, you're going to learn about modern day multihulls, their advantages and disadvantages over monohulls, and what sets catamarans apart from trimarans (besides the obvious number of hulls). With me today, I'm honored to have Jim Brown as my special guest. Hello Jim!

Jim: Good morning, Robin.

Robin: Jim, thank you so much for joining me today. Jim Brown is marine architect, multihull pioneer and builder, author, sailor, and teacher.

In the 1950s, Jim helped build the first large model molded fiberglass boats in the US. Jim built the first modern cruising trimaran and sailed it on a 2,000-mile ocean voyage with his lovely bride, Jo Anna.

In the 1960s, Jim designed the Searunner series of ocean cruising trimaran sail boats for amateur building. These designs attracted some 1,600 builders worldwide. Several of these boats have completed world cruises.

In the 1970s, Jim sailed the coasts of Central and South America with his family. He was inducted into the *Cruising World* Hall of Fame. Jim's personal yacht was selected by *Sail* magazine as one of the 100 Greatest Sailing Yachts in North America. He authored *The Case for the Cruising Trimaran,* published by

International Marine Publishing Company in 1983, which sold 11,000 copies. He also developed and patented the "constant camber" method of producing compound curved plywood modular boat components.

In the 1980s, Jim transferred constant camber technology to peasant fishermen in several remote locations in Africa, the Philippines, and the Central Pacific Islands, where it is now used to produce sophisticated working watercraft for fishing and transportation. He has written often for *WoodenBoat* and *Cruising World* magazines. He has taught wood-epoxy technology at WoodenBoat School in Brooklin, Maine.

In the 1990s, Jim was a guest lecturer on yachting history at Mystic Seaport museum and gave architectural seminars at the University of North Carolina. He designed small multihulls for mass production in rotomolded polyethylene, with thousands sold for rental and expedition service. He has voyaged to Cuba. He designed several large catamaran excursion craft, built with constant camber technology and certified by the US Coast Guard for carrying passengers on offshore routes.

Since 2000, Jim has been the recipient of an award for outstanding achievement by the New England Multihull Association. He is a cofounder of OutRig!: The Modern Multihull History Project, which collects, preserves, and disseminates the history and lore of modern seafaring. Jim is now in his late 70s and has two grown sons who are both boat designers and builders. He writes, sails, kayaks, and travels all over with Jo Anna, his wife of 51 years. They are based in rural Tidewater, Virginia. Wow, Jim, you have done a lot!

Jim: Well, that concludes my remarks for today. We don't have to go any further. (laughter)

Multihulls

Robin: Where do modern multihulls come from? What made them happen?

Jim: There are three basic multihull configurations available today. The catamaran, the trimaran, and the proa (pronounced **proh**-*uh)* all come to us from the ancient people of the South Pacific, the Indian Ocean, and even as far as west as the East Coast of Africa—all multihull territory. There are still literally hundreds of thousands of these boats in daily service on a Stone Age level. When I say that, I mean no metal parts. The ancient multihulls, which go back some say as far as three or four millennia, were made entirely of vegetable fiber. There was nothing in them that wouldn't go away with time, so there's not a whole lot known about the really ancient multihulls. There's no doubt that they've been around for a long time and the way it looks now they're going to be with us for another two or three millennia, no doubt.

The thing about these boats that a lot of people don't realized today is that they were probably the first real seafaring vessels known to mankind. Today we think of multihulls as being something new. In fact, most people think of them as just happening yesterday, but the truth is, well, if tradition means old and time tested, the multihull watercraft is probably the most traditional of all surface vessel types in the world.

Multihulls are an Asiatic concept. They began in what we would call Island Asia now and they were used in all three configurations in order to explore and eventually populate the entire Pacific basin as far north as Hawaii. It's quite something when you think about the fact that these boats were making planned ocean voyages—out one year and back the next—thousands of miles offshore at about the same time that the Venetians were just beginning to fiddle their way down around the hump of Africa always within sight of land. The ability to use the multihull was very much dependent on the early multi mariners being able to lie on deck, look up at the sky, and almost empirically locate themselves on the face of the planet.

Multihull boatbuilding is an amazing technology that goes back a long way, while our own nautical heritage is very much monohull. The multihuller was doing it before, perhaps long before, it was done off shore in monohull vessels. When you think of multihulls today, you really can't consider them something new. They've been around for a long time.

There was something that happened right after World War II. It was a classic case of reinvention that was applied to the basic configurations and I think that reinvention was materials driven. We found that a lot of materials science had advanced during World War II to the point where things like plywood and fiberglass and light metals and synthetic fibers for sail cloths and for cordage and all of those things became commonly available in the years shortly after World War II. That led to a reinvention of the multihull. These modern multihulls are not reproductions or emulations of the ancient vessels in any way. They're an entirely new breed of watercraft. The thing that really makes a modern multihull modern is light weight. There were attempts to utilize the multihull configuration by westerners going back as far as the 1600s, but the light weight did not appear until right after the war. The ancient multihulls were wonderfully light, don't get me wrong. They were wonderfully light for the materials and the tools that were available to their builders, but nothing like what can be achieved with modern materials.

So something really happened post war that made the modern multihull happen. It was not just materials driven. As I see it, the global context at the time tended to encourage the development of new stuff. After the war there was a great buoyant optimism in the developed countries. We had managed to quash the despots in Europe and Asia. We felt ourselves to be a special people, like we could do anything; with enough wealth and will, we could change the world. I think that stimulated a smattering of inventors who were working with new vessel types using modern materials in places like Australia, New Zealand, England, and, particularly, in California and Hawaii. That's really what made multihulls happen—that 'can do' generation.

I guess we began to lose that by the early '70s. We were not so buoyantly optimistic anymore. We were taking a licking in Vietnam and we had sort of given up on the idea of trying to do away with poverty and bigotry and all of that. We had a different thing enter into the multihull fold at that time—what I call 'escapism.'

Most of the early multihulls during the '40s, '50s, and '60s were built by owner-builders, not all but most of them were backyard operations by what you'd call mad scientists experimenting. Some of us saw the potential and really invested substantial portions of our lives in making this thing happen. The enthusiasm, almost hysteria, that accompanied the emergence of these boats, was definitely a result of the context of the times. I have to say, hats off to those experimenters—the guys that really led the way, the real trail blazers.

I was not one of them; I was rather a Johnny-come-lately. I got into multihulls when I was in my early 20s. I was standing on the shoulders of the guys who had really blazed the trail, who had made most of the basic discoveries in both catamarans and trimarans at that time. I was younger than most of those guys and that's one reason I'm still around. That's why I sort of feel obliged to tell the story of this incredible burst of energy and creativity that went into developing these boats early on in the postwar period. I'm delighted to be included among those guys like Woody Brown, Rudy Choy, James Wharram, Arthur Piver, and Dick Newick—those guys were the real trail blazers. I'm now trying to make sure that that legacy, the legacy of that time, doesn't become lost.

Nautical historians aren't paying much attention to multihulls because they're too new. They're not curatorial yet (laughter), but we're saving the stuff.

As I see it, that's the way modern multihulls happened.

***Robin:* When and how did you get into sailing?**

Jim: I was schooner bumming around the Caribbean in my early 20s. I didn't know quite what else to do with myself. I pretty much failed at everything else I tried and I was a skin-diving nut. The whole underwater world was just beginning to open up at that time. This was the mid-1950s and Jacques Cousteau had really made so many of us aware of 'the silent world,' as he called it.

I got myself a job on a big schooner that was carrying diving parties around the Caribbean. There was a Bahamian boatswain in the crew—we had eight guys in the crew on that boat, plus the skipper, and they were all Bahamians except for me—the boatswain, a man named Fred McKenzie, was the guy that really got me into sailing. He taught me the ways of a windjammer and it came at the right time. It just stimulated the living daylights out of me to the point where it's been one damn boat after another ever since. But it was a strong traditional background—I didn't start out in multihulls; I came out of conventional boats.

Robin: **How did you become attracted mostly to multihulls?**

Jim: It was a blind luck, pure happenstance. I found myself in the company of two very influential mentors—people that really shaped the rest of my life. One of them was a guy named Wolfgang Kraker von Schwarzenfeld. He's very little known in the annals of multihull history these days, but he was actually one of the first. He was a German guy that had been through the living hell during the war in Europe and built himself a catamaran out of tin and sailed it across the Atlantic. He was even ahead—maybe only by a matter of days—of James Wharram (British), the other real pioneer in the Atlantic. But Wolfgang crossed to the Antilles in 1956 and made his way up the islands to Miami where I met him. He was looking to join the crew of this big schooner that I was working in, the Janine, a 151-foot steel stafle schooner, a marvelous thing.

The captain of the schooner, this guy Mike Burke, who was soon to become famous as the proprietor of Windjammer

Barefoot Cruises, which really opened up the charter business in the Caribbean, needed a bunch of photographs to prepare a brochure. Wolfgang was a shutterbug, so he came into the crew. It took me a while to find out about all the circumstances that led him to cross the Atlantic in this catamaran. I later saw the boat in Miami and I must say it was the first multihull I ever saw and it offended me roundly. I couldn't get over the gruesomeness of the thing and I couldn't understand how a guy could cross the ocean in it.

So, I was interested and one thing led to another and Wolf and I and this great gal, Jeannie Miller, joined us. She was a passenger on one of the diving trips and she hit it off with Wolfgang. The three of us ended up forming a nice tight diving and sailing team. We left the schooner and took off for South America in another yacht, had some big deal adventures and all that, and finally came out of it figuring that we were going to build ourselves what we called a triple cat at the time. Wolfgang said, "The only trouble with my boat is she needs another hull in between," and that's how the trimaran came into my life.

We ended up getting stuck in Columbia with an immigration snafu and we finally built ourselves a triple cat out of oil drums in order to get out of there. We somehow managed to make it to Panama and so on. Not long after that, I found my way to California. When I left Wolfgang and Jeannie, we were all going off to do our separate things in order to accumulate the cash we needed in order to build a boat for ourselves.

One of the things we decided was we were going to build it out of fiberglass, a very new thing at the time. I learned that there was a company in Sausalito, California, a town I had never heard of, that was building the first large fiberglass products in the United States. The British were way ahead of us at that time in fiberglass technology. But, I bought a motorcycle and rode it out there and got a job at this place and learned about fiberglass. The whole thing became a sort of lead-in to bumping into the next mentor—the guy that really played a great role in my life, this man named Arthur Piver (rhymes with diver, as he used to say). Piver is now known pretty much as the father of the modern trimaran.

This was getting into 1957-1959. The catamaran had already been developed in a very modern sense by the Hawaiian catamaran concept (that's another whole story). The catamarans were ahead of the trimarans, no doubt, in the 1950s. I had the chance to try out a couple of Hawaiian catamarans and I was quite dismayed—flummoxed by so much speed with so little control. I learned later that the reason they were not all that controllable was that they were intended to be operated from the beach. They had very shallow rudders and no center boards and all that stuff. They were for carrying joy riders off the beach at Waikiki and were not really sea boats. They would just go like stink in a straight line, ripping across the ocean like a sea plane on takeoff. I was just flabbergasted by the whole thing.

When I got back to the Sausalito, I bumped into this guy Arthur Piver. He had a little trimaran that he'd whacked out in his garage. It was also rather offensive looking—just a collection of plywood boxes—but it did everything that the catamarans of the day didn't do. It would tack dependably, come about like a sailing dinghy, and really go to windward. You could really steer it down wind in big waves. We were sailing in San Francisco Bay and the Golden Gate. We had a chance to really test this thing.

So I became a protégée of Arthur Piver and that's really where I came into the multihull fold. With these little boats of his—this was a 16-footer and he had another one, a 20-footer—we'd take them out into the Golden Gate and just go blasting through conditions that would break an ordinary boat. I couldn't believe the sea-keeping properties that these things had. They were also beachable. Furthermore, they were unsinkable. I had had the experience in my schooner bumming days of sailing in a boat that was going down and I'd never gotten over it. It was obvious that these little trimarans of Arthur Piver's had the potential to be capsized but, at least, they wouldn't sink.

I figured if I had one that was a little bigger than the one we had at the time—let's put three sheets of plywood together instead of two so we'd have a 24-footer instead of a 16-footer—that I could put a little cuddy cabin on it and undertake a coastal voyage back to the Caribbean. I wanted to go back to the Caribbean—part of another long story—I'd lost track of Wolfgang and Jeannie. It would be 35 years before I would find Wolfgang again. Another thing that really attracted me to Piver's little trimarans was their low cost. Multihulls are generally more expensive to build than monohulls. But in the early days they were easy to whack out by an amateur builder. Even if you'd never even built a bird house, you could build a collection of plywood boxes and go out in the big briny and really have yourself an adventure.

I discarded the first trimaran I built before I finished it. I needed that experience to start again. I was definitely self-taught when it came to building. A lot of the builders at that time were buying plans from Arthur Piver. A lot of them were absolute green horn wood butchers—no idea what they were doing—but the boats worked. At least some of them worked, not all of them, it's true. Many builders in the early days did extraordinary improvisation in finishing off their boats and some of the craziest, wackiest floating contraptions you can imagine resulted, but the ones that were built to the plan worked pretty well. I figured that because they were beachable, that I could make a coastal voyage in this thing. Even if I got in real trouble, I could always run it in onto the beach.

That's what I eventually did with my wife Jo Anna. We built this 24-footer that Arthur Piver called Nugget and sailed it out the Golden Gate in August of 1959 and turned left and headed off for Mexico. It was nuts—absolutely the dumbest thing we ever did. Jo Anna was five and a half months pregnant by the time I got the boat built, but we decided to go anyway. It was absolutely nuts, but we pulled it off....

Robin: What a story!

Jim: I guess it's a story, but there are thousands of them, Robin. There are thousands of stories out there like that. That's what we're trying to collect now with our multihull history project. I'll tell you about that later.

Robin: **What are the advantages and disadvantages of having a multihull over a monohull?**

Jim: (laughter) In the early days, multihulls were very countercultural. There was a rather dreadful schism between the multihull people and the monohull people.

Robin: **Like the sail and the power boats today?**

Jim: It was worse than that. It was almost like the stand-off between science and religion. People that were really devoted to their boats, no matter what the type, could find plenty of ammunition to argue the issue on both sides of the table.

Is a multihull better than a monohull? I think maybe we'd better start with the disadvantages.

Disadvantages of multihulls over monohulls

What's happened to multihulls since the modern multihull early days is that they have become astronomically expensive. That was not the case in the beginning. The reason for that is the multihulls cost more to produce. The owner-builder has pretty much faded out of the picture. All these boats are being produced by front yard operations that require high investment. There's a lot of regulation involved and high expectations on the part of the clientele. They want a boat that comes out looking smooth and shiny like an automobile. It certainly does not have to be in order to sail it around the world. This has been driven partly by the clientele and the designers. There's been what Dick Newick calls this 'greed for speed.' It has driven multihulls toward high tech and high cost to the point where they've almost been driven into obscurity, particularly in today's market place where most people just can't spend the money on a modern production multihull. Of course, all of the production yacht builders today are in deep yogurt...

Robin: ...for the same reasons too—because the clientele want all these expensive fast-going boats and they're forgetting about years ago when it was just go out, relax, have fun, leave the comforts of home at home.

Jim: A lot of the stuff that's come down to us in the name of, here's another Dick Newick term, 'modern inconveniences,' has not necessarily enhanced the sailing experience.

Another part of the high cost of modern multihulls is not just their purchase, but also their maintenance. The berthing and haul-out costs and so on are usually greater than with monohulls.

That's really put the bite on the business to the point where, in fact, the entire recreational boating industry is being driven down onto trailers. Anything you can trailer is of great interest these days—you don't have to pay berth rental and you can bring it home to work on it yourself. That relates the multihulls in this way: it's pretty hard to trailer a very wide boat. There have been a number of clever means of developing trailerable trimarans and catamarans, those that fold up in order to get them onto the highway legally at their legal trailering beam. There's a lot of activity in that area today. I'm very interested in that area myself, because if you can trailer it, it also means you can build it in your garage.

At least with a smaller vessel, the age of the owner-builder is coming back. The editors of *WoodenBoat* magazine are telling me they're seeing an absolute explosion in the owner building of small wooden watercraft. That's mostly kayaks, canoes, skiffs, and stuff like that, but it's also happening in multihulls.

Robin: I've gone to the **Wooden Boat Show** and they have a **section called "I built it myself."** The boats entered into that contest are unbelievable, but there's a waiting list of over a year to be entered into that now. They can only take 50 people.

Jim: It's wonderful. It looks like the economic squeeze that we're all feeling, is driving a reemergence of the can-do generation. I love it myself. I may be just an old timer, but I love it.

There are a couple of other disadvantages now to multihulls. A major one, to my mind, is limited load carrying ability. Multihulls are not good load carriers. If the ancient Pacific multihulls had been able to carry cannons, we might be speaking another language today. The boats were so much faster and more maneuverable than the big British blunderbuss things. The European explorers that first showed up in the Pacific in 1600s were just agog at the performance of the ancient multihulls. And they had them that were big enough, like the Fiji Ndrua, the real juggernaut of the South Pacific—90-feet long, carrying 200 warriors, at 20 knots—but they couldn't carry cannons.

The trouble with multihulls is that, particularly the cruising vessels, cruising tends to encourage the pack rat. Your boat gets just stuffed full of all kinds of stuff that you think you're going to need and maybe you will someday and you'd like to be able to reach for it, but it tends to overload multihulls. The reason for that is the multihulls have narrow hulls. That's the real essence of the multihulls. Whether it's the main hull and the floats of a trimaran, or the twin hulls of the catamaran, those hulls are very narrow. That's why they go, that's why they're so fast—they don't cause that wave making phenomenon that monohulls do. Monohulls have to be wide enough to stand up on their own and multihulls don't.

In fact the design of multihulls is kind of a cop-out in a way, because the designer doesn't even have to consider what we call form stability when designing the individual hulls. You can make them narrow enough so that you put them in water they fall right over on their sides. But when you hook two or three of them together and spread them wide apart, you have something that is geometrically more stable than a monohull could be, but as the water sees the hull forms, they're still narrow. They can break through what they call that hump in the resistance curve and really take off. They just don't push a wave ahead and drag a wave behind like monohulls have to in order to be wide enough to keep from falling over, especially sailboats.

There's a real difference here in the two types. The narrow hulls just won't carry the weight. The shape of the hole that they're making in the surface of the water—when you put the narrow hull in the water, it doesn't have to push as much water out of the way to come down to its water line—that's why they go, but it's also why you can't just keep asking them to push more and more water out of the way. The real Achilles heel of multihulls is the under-wing—the underside of the bridge structure, or what we call the wing, that holds the hulls together. Whether it's two hulls or three, you've got to join them all together somehow. That structure reaches out like a big arm and holds on to the other hull, it has a surface that has to be kept up out of the wave tops. In most cruising catamarans, in particular, that under-wing surface is the real Achilles heel of the boat. If the waves get big enough or you push the boat fast enough, or if you push it down in the water deep enough, that under-wing starts to take a real licking by the wave tops.

That pounding on the under-wing and the limited load carrying are the real disadvantages to multihulls. You can work around them. You have to change your mind about what you're going to take along with you and sometimes you have to change your mind about which way you're going to go against the wind. You'll slow down or bear off or do something to reduce the pounding, which is particularly bad in the big catamarans. The hulls are spaced wide enough apart so that they can actually straddle a wave crest. Let's say the weather hull passes over the crest and starts down the back of the wave, and the crest is still there and it slams on the under wing before it lifts up the leeward hull to get over the crest. That pounding business is a real limitation. It means you just can't take everything you want to. It also means that the modern catamaran is at a particular disadvantage. I'll try to talk about that later, but let's get to the advantages, ok?

Advantages of multihulls over monohulls

Speed: personally, I never have thought that speed was the primary advantage of the multihull, but a lot of people think of them as being fast and of course we now know that they can do such wonderful things. The latest big French trimarans are crossing the ocean in three or four days—faster than ocean liners. The America's Cup vessels recently were able to turn in speed in the recent contest between the big catamaran and the big trimaran, the Oracle and the Alinghi. Those boats in their practice sessions, were regularly flirting with 50 knots of boat speed. They can go very fast, even in very light airs. They can be driven hard in light airs because their rigs are so powerful. Those things can sail almost four times faster than the wind is blowing.

Speed is one advantage, even in the cruising boat that's overloaded and was never intended to go fast. There's nothing wrong with just darn well getting where you're going. Some sailors that buy big pudgy monohulls are saying, "The last thing I want to do is hurry. I go out, I'm going sailing to relax and float." But you're going to expose yourself to a lot more discomfort out there than if you had a boat that would lope along at half again as fast. That's about the kind of speed I talk about— a cruising multihull should be able to knock out speeds about half again as fast as an equivalent cruising monohull. Some multihulls will go a whole lot faster than that, but they've come up with some very fast monohulls these days. Multihulls have driven the advance of sailing technology. The potential for that speed that was demonstrated by early multihulls have driven a lot of marine architecture ever since World War II.

The next advantage of multihulls is motion. The multihull *can* have a motion that's less comfortable than the equivalent monohull, but most of the time it's far *more* comfortable. If you have an equivalent monohull and multihull anchored in the same roadstead and it's a quiet day, but the harbor is all chopped up with motorboat wakes, the multihull is going to jump around more than the monohull. But if it's an open roadstead and there's a real swell running through, it can easily cause the monohull to roll its rails down—just roll your eyeballs out. Whereas, the multihull sits there like a duck and bobs up and down over the surface and has to conform to the shape of the wave. It's definitely not immobile, but doesn't develop that residual pendulum type roll motion that monohulls do. While underway, particularly at speed, they can be marvelously smooth riding—not all of them are, that's for sure, but they can be.

Then the interiors—the modern cruising catamarans, in particular, have these glorious accommodations. They can be so much like your recreation room at home that inexperienced people look at them and say that's what I want. Most of the bridge cabin catamarans of today have this wonderful communal space in the bridge. It might have the whole galley there, together with lots of lounging area, the navigation station, entertainment, books, the whole thing, is there in this bridge cabin that is held up by the hulls of the catamaran.

But here comes the problem, there is so much space in them, that sometimes the design is not intended for real seafaring. The designer is encouraged to reduce the under-wing clearance that I was talking about before to gain standing headroom in the bridge cabin. You can see that the crew that's now waltzing around in the bridge cabin has its feet well above the waterline if the boat is any good. That means you have to push up the superstructure, the house top begins to develop a lot of what a sailor calls top hamper—it's very well named. Many cruising catamarans have, in my view, unacceptable top hamper. It's what my friend Joe Hudson called the school bus effect, done in order to provide these glorious accommodations, but it tends to push the under-wing down and the house top up.

When the multihull gets big enough—some say 50 feet, I think 60 feet is a better number—you can deal with that; you can have enough under-wing clearance *and* enough headroom in the bridge to make a good boat out of it without it becoming excessively school bus-y. In so many cruising catamarans, the helmsman's position—the actual pilot seat of the boat—has to be on a double-high bar stool behind the school bus so you can see over it. The helmsman is perched up there in a fighting chair that if he falls out of, he's got a long way to get down to the under-wing. You see a lot of modern multihulls that are designed that way and many of them are good for just what they are intended for—lakes, bays, rivers, and sounds—protected water. But if you're going to go out in the big briny, you've got to have under-wing clearance and that's hard to do in a small catamaran.

All the exhibitors showing their modern cruising catamarans at the boat shows should provide a kayak in the water, so that the prospective buyer can get into the kayak and see if he can get his way under the wing of the boat. If you can paddle a kayak through the tunnel of a catamaran, you got a pretty good boat. For a small cat, you might have to scrunch down, bend and put your head between your knees, in order to get through there. But you see some of them at boat shows where you can barely see through there. A lot of them have these big protuberances that stick down and out of the bottom of the wing or out of the side of the hulls that really detract from their seafaring nature, in my view. Normally speaking, the modern catamaran can have wonderful interiors, but the trimarans can too, it's just a different sort of interior. You don't have that big block of space in the middle of the boat that resembles your living room at home. The accommodations are more like in a monohull—maybe we can speak to that later.

The other real advantage to a multihull over monohull, in my opinion, is safety. That's not been their classic reputation. We were roundly criticized in the early days of multihulls. We were told that we were going to sea in a boat that would make us swim for our lives. That might well be true if one is looking only at the prospect of capsize, but you can't look only at the prospect of capsize, you have to compare it with the prospect of sinking. We've learned that the two are very similar. Sinking and capsize are both very rare in the cruising boats these days. Capsize is quite common in the racers, but no more common than racing monohulls that have their keels break off or their hulls break in half. And there are the other very common kinds of marine hazards—collisions, fire, shipwreck, stranding…

Robin: …and running aground is a big one now.

Jim: We'll get to shoal draft, boy—that's one of the main advantages of multihulls. But just because you have shoal draft doesn't mean you're not going to run aground. You start sneaking around in thin water and you'll find yourself stuck more often than if you had a deep boat. The great thing about that is you can step off and push the boat off the bar and climb back on again and keep going. I have an old 31-foot trimaran that whenever we run aground, my sons and I just jump out and push off.

The common kinds of accidents, particularly shipwrecks where the boat is stranded, we have many examples of the crew living through calamitous shipwrecks and ending up being able to just step off onto dry land with the multihulls. That doesn't happen with monohulls, boy. The keel hits the reef and the boat lies over on its side and gets a hole poked in it with seas bursting over the upturned bilge and the crew is really isolated a long way from land.

In collision, most multihulls are unsinkable and that's a tremendous safety advantage. When you start thinking about that, thousands of years of sailing have accepted the possibility of sinking. We sort of likely go to sea, try to prepare for it, and try to prevent it.

The same thing has to be done with capsize—there's no doubt about it. The real difference between capsize and sinking is the consequence of capsize is much preferred to the consequence of sinking. We find that multihulls, particularly trimarans, can provide a habitat for the castaway sailors after an offshore capsize. You compare that with a sunken monohull where the boat literally disappears from the face of the earth, and you've got to concede that non-sinking multihulls have a tremendous safety advantage if you're going to take it all the way to zero hour.

Robin: You've convinced me.

Jim: It took us a long time to convince ourselves. I had this thing about sinking because I'd almost been through it. So maybe I was little more open to the notion than most people, but, boy, most traditional sailors thought that we early multihullers were just nuts to go offshore in that thing.

The real advantage—and I'll concede that this is the one point that cannot be argued from both sides of the table (all the other points I've made in the way of advantages can be argued by a monohull aficionado)—the one thing that the multihull has that cannot be approached in a monohull is they've been developed now to the point where they have these splendid seakeeping properties. That is combined with shoal draft. In no other configuration do you get that combination to that extent. That just gives a cruising sailor a crack at another whole hemisphere of the water planet that is inaccessible to the offshore sailor with a deep boat. You can't argue against that.

If I could close the discussion of advantages and disadvantages, I might say that the real difference between multihulls and monohulls is in their people. The people who are willing to embrace the multihull concept are really embracing a different attitude toward the sea, Robin. It's another way of looking at it. I'm not saying that one boat is better than another, I'm not. I still love monohulls. I think a sailing dingy is the niftiest thing around. Monohulls, in my view, get really good when they get big—50 feet's okay, but 150 feet is great—you've got a great thing there. It's just that I could never afford one.

But this attitude toward the sea is based on a new generation of humanity. Many of today's water people came out of swim fins and masks and snorkels and surf boards and wind surfers. It's a whole different thing. These guys look at a big wave as not a threat, but as something to be enjoyed. They don't consider their boats to be a fortress to protect them against the sea. They're more like an implement that they can use in order to go out there and really get it on, really jam through the waves. It's an entirely different attitude toward the sea, I think. That's a lot of blah-blah, but that's the way I see the differences, the two types.

Robin: That is a huge difference.

Jim: Yeah, a lot of people don't think about all that stuff. I've been thinking about it a lot lately, of course, because I've been trying to write a book about it. I'll tell you about that later if you're interested.

Robin: **Aside from the obvious fact that catamarans have two hulls and trimarans have three, what else sets them apart, given both their advantages and disadvantages? I know you mentioned a lot of it earlier with the multihull over the monohull. But there must be some differences between the catamaran and the trimaran.**

Jim: There are some more distinctions that apply to the configurations. They really are different animals. Because the world is gone cat crazy, Robin, there are a lot of people out there that don't even think trimarans are multihulls, they're something else off the wall, some other kind of creature. But, if we want to stay with this biological metaphor, we could say that both catamarans and trimarans come from the same phylum. They're both surface watercraft. The catamarans and the trimarans are different than most other watercraft because they have more than one torso or thorax or whatever you want to call it. They're quite different creatures relative to monohulls. The difference between the cat and the tri is they're distinctly different species, but in the same phylum and the same genus.

First of all, there are structural differences because of this configuration thing. The trimaran, with its big central main hull and its two smaller outer hulls or outrigger hulls, is conceptually a little easier to deal with structurally. In fact, probably the first real multihulls that ventured offshore were trimarans—the good old double outrigger canoe. It's easy to tie floats onto a main hull, but it's not too easy to tie two main hulls together—they're bigger and heavier, you've got more going on there.

In the trimaran (let's come to the modern trimaran now), the main hull provides you with things that you don't get with the cat, structural things. One of them is the place to step the mast. In a catamaran it's pretty hard to find a place to step the mast without having an enormously strong bridge reaching across between the two boats. You also get a place in the trimaran to attach the head stay or jib stay out on the bow. You don't have a bow out there in the catamaran, not on center. The catamaran also requires two rudders, it's not strictly true, but most catamarans have twin rudders and you have to hook them together somehow. The steering linkages get to be very involved and expensive in cats. The two centerboards—the centerboard and its trunks—have to be duplicated in the catamaran, not in the trimaran.

And here's the biggie—the trimaran can get along just fine on one engine. Whereas the catamaran, well, you can run a catamaran with one engine and you can run a catamaran with one centerboard, but that's not the way to do it and most people don't do it that way. So, you can save a lot of weight and cost in the trimaran, because of its main hull to attach the jib stay, the centerboard, the rudder, and the engine.

In the catamaran, the other structural differences also come into play. You almost have to have a model in front of you to look them over in order to really get a handle on it. The bridge between the hull, these differences relate to the size of the several hulls in a single vessel—their size and their spacing, how wide apart they are. The catamaran has twin hulls, they're both the same size and they're spaced rather wide apart. It's a long way from one hull to the other in the catamaran. Whereas in the trimaran, unless you make it extremely wide, and that's what they're doing to the race boats now, the space between the main hull and the outer hull is somewhat less than in the catamaran.

These differences, well it gets to be pretty complex to talk about it, but I've already mentioned one in the big cats especially, with the hulls wide apart, they can straddle the wave crest and cause pounding on the under-wing. In the trimaran, the harder you drive it, the more you push the lee hull down and the closer to the water comes the under-wing panel.

So there are disadvantages to both types when it comes to their hull spacing. The trimaran's float hull or outer hull is not as far away from the main hull—there's not as much room in there—but you do push the lee hull down. There are other factors that we call interplay wave making. The early trimarans were not wide enough to avoid the problem of the main hull bow wave angling off and running into the float. Now they're made wide enough so as we can avoid that problem.

But, I hasten to say that all of these structural differences, all of the problems of one type or another, have now been overcome. There's no doubt that you can make a good strong catamaran, even though there's no simple place to attach the head stay. The same thing with trimarans—I mean, if you only have one engine, maybe someday you're going to wish you had two because one won't work. It's the old trade off. There is so much compromise that goes on in marine design of all types of vessels, both monohull and multihull.

Basically, we can say that catamarans are better load carriers than trimarans. They have two big hulls instead of one. If a trimaran is a good one, it's designed so that its float hulls are actually held up pretty much out of the water by the main hull. The main hull has to carry the load of the outrigger hulls in the trimaran. The reason for that is if you push the outer hulls down too deep in the trimaran, it cuts into their maneuverability. That is, you have to drag the full length of three hulls through the turn while tacking and that's when the power is turned off.

That's another difference, the catamaran has to drag its two hulls through the tack. The trimaran, if it's properly designed, basically only has to drag one hull through the tack. For that reason, trimarans are more maneuverable than catamarans. It's easier to tack them; it's easier to sail a snake wake through the harbor and avoid traffic and stuff like that in the trimaran. They're quicker on the helm, generally speaking; not strictly true, but generally speaking.

Yet the catamaran is better on the beach. If you're to beach the boat, voluntarily or by accident, the catamaran, if indeed you have a sandy beach or even if you don't, the thing will sit there like a big raft on the beach. Whereas the trimaran, its main hull is deeper and if you've got any surf running as a swash on the beach, the trimaran will lurch drunkenly from one float to the other as it responds to the surf while pivoting on the main hull, which is the only thing that's aground.

Most people would say that the catamaran has better accommodations. We've talked about that. In my view, that point is arguable. The catamaran has accommodations that are better for those who regard their boats as domiciles. The trimaran has better accommodations for those who regard their boats as vehicles. There's a real tradeoff to be made there and a lot of thinking that needs to be invested by the prospective buyer, designer, or builder, because right in there, a lot happens. So many people buy a boat because of its accommodations. Well, what kind of accommodations are we talking about here? Do you want to be a good live-aboarder in the marina? Or you want to spend months at a time in the various harbors that you go and visit? Or do you want your boat to be a gin palace where you can have all your friends come down on the weekends and hang out? If so, maybe you'd better have a catamaran. But if you want to get out there on the big briny, particularly with a small crew, and have a really good place to fix your meals, do your navigating, and all of that, in a way that is private and apart from the crew, the off-watch that's trying to rest, maybe you'd better think about a trimaran.

Trimarans are also better upwind, Robin. It's not universally true, of course, because it depends on the boat itself, but, generally speaking, trimarans are better up wind and that's because their centerboards or dagger boards are mounted in the main hull. The main hull of the trimaran is deeper than the hulls of a catamaran, so the centerboard starts from deeper and goes deeper. It can reach down there into solid, quiet water and hang on. Also, being in the center, it contributes to the steering properties of the boat.

And there are other aspects, differences between these two animals that make the trimaran a better boat up wind. It relates to motion—I'm talking now about the comparison in the size and the spacing of the hulls. The catamaran hulls are the same size. Each one of them has to be big enough to support the entire weight of the boat if you were to stand the boat on edge. It has to be a lot bigger than that, actually. The trimaran, on the other hand, its outer hulls are of different size than the main hull. Their gross displacement, when buried to the deck, can be adjusted by the designer so as to make it possible for the sailor to see very clearly when his boat is being overdriven.

The catamaran, because it's so darn stable, especially the big ones, it's just incredible, it's like going offshore in a pool table. You've got 10-foot waves that are rolling around and you walk around the decks with your hands in your pockets. It's just amazing how stable they are. And yet, if the wind blows hard enough or the wave gets big enough, you can pick up the weather hull without depressing the leeward hull much. That makes the catamaran, in my view, less intuitive, less user-friendly.

The trimaran will communicate with the pilot in a much more direct manner. It will tell you in no uncertain terms that you're driving the daylights out of your boat, because the lee float, the bow of the downwind outrigger, will go driving right through the crests. That's normal behavior when driving the boat hard to windward. You don't push the whole float underwater, you push just the bow, and you see the crest rolled down the deck. But you still got maybe half of the buoyancy of the lee float still out of the water, and it's telling you, "Hey, man! Do you want to really do this?" Okay—you've got a good strong crew, guys that know what they're doing. You're driving for the finish mark in a race, and you got another boat that's trying to put you in its lee. Okay—strap it down and let her go. Lash that bugger—let her go. But not when you're offshore. You don't behave like that offshore, unless you're one of these hard bitten racers who go to bed while the boat is doing that.

I personally think that single-handed racing is unseamanlike because the boat has to be operated at flank speed very often with no one on watch. Even at times like that, the trimaran is more communicative with the pilot than the catamaran. They're a little more user-friendly in that way and for that reason, I think they're more like a monohull and they're less likely to become capsized than the catamaran because they tell the sailor when it's driving too hard.

The cat appeals to inexperienced sailors, but people who are coming out of monohulls can understand the trimaran a little better. You can get down in the middle and put your feet below the waterline and still have standing headroom without putting the school bus on deck.

That whole business of intuitive, user-friendly operation, I think that argument has to go to the trimaran but only for boats that are really intended for serious offshore operation. I think also that the trimarans are safer.

Here's a real distinction: not only are they less likely to become capsized, in my view, but they're also habitable when capsized and a catamaran is not. And the reason for that is when the trimaran is capsized, the outer hulls form giant airlock spaces. They are air tanks and they will hold the main hull up high enough to make the interior of the main hull habitable even when the boat's upside down. You can cut a hole in the hull or open the safety hatch in that capsized trimaran in order to ventilate, to get oxygen inside the main hull, while the vessel is capsized. With the catamaran, if you violate the airlock that's in those capsized hulls, the boat is probably going to settle too deep to be habitable inside.

So, like a sunken monohull that has disappeared, the catamaran requires that the crew take to a life raft. I'm not saying that they should take to the life raft alone. It becomes critical now for the life raft to remain tethered to the mother ship in a catamaran. We've had several incidents to indicate that it's a bad mistake to take off in your life raft if you can stay attached to your capsized mother ship, because the mother ship contains all kinds of stuff that you can use for survival while awaiting rescue. There are a number of wonderful historic examples to illustrate that point, Robin. We've seen it, particularly with my great friend, John Glennie, who with his crew of two managed to survive for 120 days—four months—inhabiting their capsized trimaran in the South Pacific. When they finally got to the shore, they were in such good shape that the authorities didn't believe their story.

If you want to talk about safety, that's ultimate safety—that's zero hour—that's the very thing that really niggles the mind of the man, woman, child who is contemplating sailing offshore. "My G-d, what if the thing sinks or capsizes?" From what we know about it now, you'd rather have it capsize, and if it's going to do that, you'd rather have it be a trimaran and a catamaran, at least that's my analysis. It's pretty longwinded; I hope somebody is still interested, because I think this is hot stuff.

Robin: This is just fascinating.

Jim: We've learned a lot in the last 50 years. A lot of it we've learned the hard way; a lot of us have learned our seamanship the hard way. There have been a lot of crack ups, some loss of life, and some true tragedy in order to accumulate this knowledge. But we've got it now, and there's just no doubt, Robin, that it all points to the fact that multihulls represent an absolute sea change in marine architecture. We're going to see a whole lot more of them, both recreational and commercial, and military—no doubt in my mind.

Robin: I know quite a few people now that are actually buying cats. I don't know so many buying trimarans, but I know a few that are building their own. It is heading that way.

Jim: That could be a pretty hard nail to get into trimarans because the press these days—the evidence in the harbor and so on—is mostly catamaran. There's no doubt that, for most of what they're used for, they're just great. Cats are great. Cats are great for these excursion vessels, what we call the cattle-marans that carry joy riders off the beaches and all the warm water resorts all around the world now. Those cats are just great; they've got great big ones now. The largest I've designed was 64 feet. One of those was certified by the Coast Guard for a 150 passengers and they steam the thing right up to the beach and pick the people up right out of the surf. They drop a ladder down between the bow nets and people can walk out of their hotels, scramble up on the boat, and go out and watch the whales and the birds and the sky and the mountains. Charter catamarans are a big deal and cats seem to be better at it than trimarans.

Robin: We've come so far in boating. **Jim, we've been talking about multihulls—catamarans and trimarans—but we haven't yet talked about a proa. What's that?**

Jim: Proa (pronounced **proh-***uh*) is one of the words used in the ancient South Pacific to describe a vessel that some people call a half a trimaran. That is, it has one main hull and only one smaller outrigger hull. To be a true proa, that contraption has to carry that outrigger hull always on one side or the other, usually on the windward side; that is, the outrigger hull—the small hull—to windward. The reason for that is that the rig of the boat is set up so that it can accept the wind only from one side.

This sounds absolutely nuts and proas really are off the wall. We're getting into some pretty zany stuff here. Keeping the small hull always to windward, let's say to windward—some of them keep it always to leeward; never in the ancient boats, but some of the modern boats, such as the so-called Atlantic trimaran, as designed by Dick Newick, carry the outrigger hull on the downwind side, but the ancient Pacific boats and most of the other proas carry their outrigger hull on the upwind side— what this means is that you can't tack. If you tack, the wind comes around on the other side of the vessel and there's nothing to hold the rig up. If you tack through the eye of the wind, the wind changes sides.

Let's say you're on the port tack and the wind's coming in over your left ear, and you want to tack, so you put the boat up through the wind and come around and you're on a starboard tack and you've got the wind coming over your right ear. You can't do that with the proa, not the same way. What you have to do instead is stop and put the other end forward. They sail either end first and it's pretty hard to describe this but it's not called tacking, it's called shunting. A true proa must be able to shunt; it cannot tack. Let's say you're going along here on what you might call the port tack and the outrigger is off on your left side there and you're sailing along and you want to go off on the other "tack" (we called it the other shunt), instead of turning left through the eye of the wind, you turn right and stop and adjust the sails so as to make what was the stern now the bow.

Robin: That's a lot of skill.

Jim: It's culturally outlandish for, because we think of boats as being bilateral, having a right side and a left side, like we have a right ear and a left ear.

Robin: **How do they get anywhere? It sounds time consuming.**

Jim: It is until you get a handle on it. You get a handle on it and you realize that except in one peculiar predicament, the proa is really a lot more manageable and maneuverable than the tacking vessel. We could go on and on about this, Robin, and I'm afraid it's a subject for another time, but I'll summarize by saying that there's a lot going on in proas today. It's like the early days of catamarans and trimarans. We have some very can-do experimenters out there, pushing the envelope toward the proa. I have absolutely no doubt that the proa has a lot to show us yet. It's going to take at least as much of a mind shift as from monohull to multihull for us to embrace the proa. I'm not willing to bet on it yet, but I wouldn't be a bit surprised, I don't know that I'll live to see it, but I think that the commercial vessel of the future, the commercial sail-assisted or a motor-assisted ocean-crossing watercraft of the future, is going to be a proa.

I'll have to leave it at that unless we could sit down with some drawings or a model or I could get together some of my video footage and try to illustrate how a proa operates. I happen to have the unique experience of having sailed in a true seafaring proa and understanding them pretty well because of the work of my son, Russell. He's probably the only American who has really done a lot of seafaring in the proa. I've learned from him. I had to pass the torch to do it, but I think I understand what I'm talking about with proas. I've never designed one and I would not feel myself qualified, but there's no doubt that it has a lot to show us yet. An interesting thing, here's another aspect of the proa, it was probably the multihull type that was used for exploring the Pacific by the early island people, Micronesians and Polynesians—the proa was the vessel of exploration.

The trimaran, the double outrigger canoe was probably the first seagoing multihull type because it was used for carrying people from island Asia out to the nearby island groups like the Philippines, for instance. They were pushed out by population pressures and other things. But when in came time that the Philippines too—that's 8,000 islands—was also outstripped as far as its environment was concerned—and this all happened before Christ—the people had to push out into the open Pacific and against the wind. It was the superior weatherliness of the proa that made it possible for these Stone Age vessels to explore the entire Pacific basin and for the navigator priests to come back and tell people that, "Okay, we've had logs floating in from over there for a long time and we found the island. It's over there and I can get you back to it." Then they used the catamaran as the freighter, the vessel of colonization, in order to go populate. They populated a wider area of earth than any other race at that time. That's where the proa fits in, I think.

Proas are incredibly weatherly vessels, even the old ones that were made entirely out of sticks and string. A modern proa will go to windward like you wouldn't believe. I think it's going to be possible to develop them to be the safest of all offshore watercraft. Maybe I shouldn't say this, but the potential is there for the proa to become self-righting. If it gets knocked down, the potential is there for it to come back up. No other multihull can do that. Monohulls can do that, but they can sink. There are some interesting comparisons in there. We could talk a lot more about proa at another time if you want to.

Robin: Sounds good. **How easy would it be for a boater to switch from a monohull to a multihull?**

Jim: It wasn't easy for me. I had this strong traditional yachting background. The first multihull I saw, I was truly offended by the thing. I had to be led by the nose. My old friend Wolfie, and then Arthur Piver, they dragged me over tradition past into multihull territory. I think that would be true of many experienced sailors—people who have some sea time behind them—they'll probably have to be dragged by the nose. I've seen a lot of examples of that, particularly my dear friend Doug Jane, who had more sea time on monohulls than you can imagine and is now a great multihull proponent, but I had to work on him for years. He's now built five big ones and has done a lot of delivery passages in them and stuff like that. It *does* happen to experienced sailors, but it's easier for inexperienced sailors to embrace the multihull notion. They see that space in there, especially for wives and children and older folks—you can get around on a big catamaran with your wheelchair.

That applies particularly to the type of catamaran wherein the perspective buyer is more interested in the domicile aspects of the boat—the thing as a floating home, a cabin in the pines that you don't have to buy land for and you can move anytime you want. That's the real market for modern production cruising, recreational multihull—people that would like to have a space on the water where they can go and hang out. With this boat, they can move it. Wherever they put it, they have to pay to leave it there, and the marinas are clogged with multihulls now.

I just returned from the Rio Dulce in Guatemala which is one of the great cruising harbors in the world, I think. When my wife and my boys and I were in there in the mid-1970s, for a while we were the only cruising boat in the whole river system. It's a grand inland waterway system. I just went back with my old friend Joe Hudson. We sailed down there in his beautiful 35-foot Marples-designed trimaran. We sailed in there and learned that there are over 2,000 cruising yachts in the Rio Dulce now. It's just incredible. When you go around and look at them, which you can do—you can get your dugout canoe, put a motor on it, and run around the whole river system looking at all these boats—a lot of them are big cats and a few are tris. I didn't make a count, but I would say 20-25% of those 2,000 boats are multihulls. People park them in the Rio Dulce during hurricane season because the place is hurricane proof, and they head for the Caribbean after that.

The other great thing about the Rio Dulce is that it gives you access to the Guatemalan highlands—still the most exotic place ever I've been. My wife and I agree on that and we've been around a bit. My poor buddy Joe wants to sell his Marples now (his body has given up on him). Whoever gets it will be right in the heart of the best cruising ground in this hemisphere, I think—the Belize Keys, the Honduras Bay Islands, oh man.

Robin: Sounds wonderful. **Have any experienced sailors actually changed back to monohulls?**

Jim: Oh, I didn't talk about that (laughter). They have, yes. Some of the very most experienced sailors that I know have reversed the cycle. It's particularly true of people who are getting on in years and who don't want to have so darn much of their net worth tied up in the boat itself.

There are so very many good cruising monohulls around that are begging for ownership. You can buy a wonderful boat, spend a little money fixing it up, and have an absolute jewel of a used monohull. But you can't buy a good used catamaran that way very often, very seldom. The people that have them paid so darn much for them, they want to hang on to them. But I've had people change back, yes. I suppose we should ask them about that—why they've done that. Maybe that's a possibility for another gab here someday, Robin. I can think of a couple of people we can talk to about that—some very experienced cruising sailors who have changed back from multihull to monohull.

Another advantage of multihulls is load carrying. For the same length of boat they can carry a lot more weight and can squeeze it into a tighter spot, whether it's at the marina, the anchorage, or the boat yard.

Robin: You can **trailer it** probably a little easier.

Jim: I was thinking of larger live-aboard cruisers. A trailerable multihull is, by nature, pretty small. Ian Farrier has designed some big folding trimarans using his fascinating folding system, up to 40-footers now. They can't trailer them down the highway folded without a special permit. They have to have a lead car, a wide load sign, and all that stuff in order to get down the highway. But, just to get them into a travel lift crane for hauling out and for storing them into boat yard, it's worth it for them to fold it up.

Robin: **Is there a length restriction in multihulls, especially for racing?**

Jim: I don't think there's a restriction, except cost. As a good example, we can see, particularly in the racing boats, the big French trimarans, most of the trans-ocean speed records now are held by trimarans. They've got them up to 150 feet long—they're incredible things. The America's Cup was sailed in 90-footers. The commercial future of multihulls, which is assured now, I mean it's assured that a large part of the commercial fleet of the future is going to be on more than one hull—anything that carries lightweight cargoes—they're no good for carrying oil or ore or something like that—but, for carrying things like people and vehicles, such as in ferrying, the best of the modern fast ferries are now trimarans. They are 400 feet long and carry 1,000 passengers and 260 cars at 40 knots with unprecedented energy efficiency. That's the writing on the wall, Robin, right there. When it gets time for us to give up flying and driving frivolously, which appears now to be inevitable, the way to get across the water is definitely going to be in the modern multihulls. Look how far they've come in the last 50 years. Give us *another* 50 years and I think the trans-ocean liners are going to be motor-sailors. We can talk more about that someday, too.

Robin: We can, but we won't be around to see it. **How do things like displacement beam and sail area relate to stability and performance in multihulls?**

Jim: We're getting pretty technical here.

Robin: We have some technical listeners.

Jim: It's enough to say that they do relate. The designer uses them in the form of ratios and there's a thing we call the displacement to speed ratio, displacement to length ratio, displacement to sail area ratio, which is more to your question. All of those things are numbers that a designer can come up that allow him to compare the boat that he's designing with other boats that have known performance features. It's a fascinating juggling act.

It does relate to stability for sure, and to instability. All of that relates to performance. Without getting into a course on marine architecture, which I'm not qualified to teach, we'd just better say that there's no magic in mulithulls. There's no designer mumbo jumbo that other designers don't have, because they haven't done multihulls yet. You do have to learn how to use a few things a little differently. We have thousands of prototype multihulls out there sailing around, and a lot of data on them.

Actually, some of the new ones are really beginning to gather a lot of data. We can see just how tightly integrated the subject of marine design is. In a way it's a little tighter in multihulls. If you change one thing, it seems to change everything else, and that's pretty hard to make an amateur client understand. If you're designing a boat for a guy and you say, "Now we've got to do a very careful weight study. I need to know about everything you're going to put on this boat, and I mean *everything*." So you go down the list and you come up with a total and say, "Okay, if you're going to put all of this crud on this boat, we're going to have to design it like this in order to carry that weight." And then in the middle of the construction, the guy decides that he wants a double sliding glass door.

Robin: Or he changes spouses or friends, so there's a weight difference there.

Jim: The basic ratio that speaks to your question is the *power to weight ratio*—the sail area to displacement ratio—how much power have you got held up there in the wind relative to how much weight you're trying to push through the water. You really have to push in the water. Man, you've got to push the water out of the way to get through, and water is heavy. The modern construction methods have made it possible for us to really get the weight down, at least in the racing boats, and the power way up, by building things like the rigid wing sail that was on the BMW Oracle, the America's Cup winner. It had a rigid wing sail larger than the wing on any passenger carrier in a carrying aircraft. The power that that thing generated was just astounding, and yet the boat is extremely light weight because it's all made out of carbon fiber with a great deal of very advanced engineering involved. It was wide as it was long—90 feet wide, for Pete's sake—could barely get it through the Panama Canal. That thing just had a favorable power to weight ratio—it was able, most of the time, to sail away from the competition, which was also a very advanced boat—the Swiss Alinghi catamaran. Both of those projects were splendid achievements and a lot more needs to be said about them. But the ability to manipulate these relationships, these ratios, between various factors in the design, is becoming more and more sophisticated.

It's way beyond me. I still like the idea of taking a dugout canoe and putting a couple of bamboo canes across it—a couple of little floats out there—I can understand that. Modern multihull design is becoming very advanced, no doubt. There's no magic in it, but there are a few things to learn. The biggest thing is that when you change one factor, and all those relationships, it changes everything else. The computer will tell you so. You can see it clearly when you ask, "What if…?" It's very clear. This is a red flag to the client that goes to a designer for a custom multihull design. Once you cast that thing in concrete, you damn well better not go messing with it or you're going to end up with a joke. It has happened too many times.

Robin: How do multihulls generally hold up in heavy weather? We've already talked about capsizing and the possibility of sinking compared to sinking in monohulls.

Jim: We used to a have a lot of structural problems, but they weren't of the sort that you'd expect. There's been very little record of multihulls becoming dismembered, that is, the crossbeam structure failing and allowing the hulls to fall apart. It's happened, but very little of that has gone on. It's been mostly dismastings and rudder failures, centerboard failures, and panel failures—that is, the skin of the hull and/or the under-wing is often designed to be so very light weight in order to make the boat go fast, that it doesn't do very well when resisting cyclic loads. They're not as fatigue resistant as the initial numbers seemed to suggest. So structurally speaking, we've had to learn to make monohulls stronger and stronger. Unfortunately, that means more weight, money, and work. But we've had to do it if we want the boats to last very long.

Many of the racers aren't really intended to last very long, though, over time, cyclic loads and slamming loads—the pounding business—can really raise hell on any structure. We've been slapped in the face about that more than once. So what we've got going on now is pretty darn good. You can really depend on your boat if you use it wisely—use it for what it was intended. If you take a big box and take it offshore, there's no doubt you can pound the under-wing out. But, there's a lot of evidence to suggest that when these fleets of yachts get caught offshore, such as when a whole bunch of boats are going off in a race, and terrible gale comes through, I mean truly terrible gales that have, at least twice now, caught whole fleets of yachts offshore, with the fleets composed of both multihulls and monohulls. The results of those zero-hour situations suggest that you're better off in a multihull. The multihulls come through just fine.

Robin: It's just mind boggling how they even survive, any of them, in those races.

Jim: It is. It's kind of nuts to go out there.

Robin: Exhilarating, it sounds like.

Jim: The Australians, even if they got a gale warning coming up, they'll fire the gun for a big race and send everybody out there in that stuff. I think it's downright poor seamanship. I'm not a big fan of racing. I've always thought that the real benefit of a multihull was that the thing was capable of such wonderful speeds, but when you're placing yourself in harm's way, you just throttle back so that you've got plenty of speed held in reserve.

Now, you've got to have a pretty safe boat. It's like having a good car that would go down the highway and be stable at 150 miles an hour.… Some of these modern automobiles—same with some of these trimarans and catamarans—are capable of such incredible speed. In the name of racing, they just sail them without reserve. If you take a good car and just throttle it back to 90 instead of 120 mph, it's a very safe machine, very road-worthy. The same thing is true of sea worthiness in multihulls. I've always thought that that was the real advantage of having a fast boat is that you could hold a lot of that in reserve, especially when you've got your wife and kids and all that stuff out there in a race.

Robin: One thing we haven't talked about yet is the **trimarans fitted with hydrofoils**. I see those popping up in the new magazines now.

Jim: Hydrofoils have been responsible for some of these incredible record-setting dashes that the French have made across the Atlantic and around the world; the British too. The boats you're referring to are racing trimarans fitted with what are called J foils. There are also T foils and ladder foils; different types of foils. But the J foil is like a big dagger board that's mounted in the floats of one of these extremely wide trimarans. It's a dagger board that goes down through the deck of the float and out the bottom, but at a diagonal. That is, it enters through the outboard side of the deck, let's call it the deck of the outboard hull, and comes out the bottom of that hull on its inboard side, so that it angles back underneath toward the boat.

A hydrofoil is an underwater wing and accomplishes the same thing in water than an airplane wing does in air. It's just that water is 600 or 700 times more dense than air, so the hydrofoil doesn't have to be nearly as big as the airfoil in order to generate a whole lot of lift. On these big French trimarans that carry these J foils—they're called J foils because their dagger boards are not straight, they're curved in a big arc, so if you look at the end of them, they have the shape of the letter J—when you start pushing them through the water fast enough they generate enough lift to allow these sailors (and these guys are true athletes) to drive these big trimarans, some of them 150 feet long, hard enough to lift the main hull, not just the weather hull, up out of the water and also lift most of the lee hull out of the water.

Robin: I've seen incredible photos of that in some of the sailing magazines.

Jim: They're just amazing. What that does, of course, is gets most of the boat out of the water so it can go faster. But it's a real balancing act, Robin. What they are doing is balancing that whole boat—it's a huge contraption—on that foil. The lee hull is in the water just enough along the surface to provide fore and aft stability, so the boat doesn't dive its bow or its stern. That's all the lee float is for when these boats are flying on that J foil. They don't always have conditions that'll permit that kind of sailing, but when they do, the boats can just take off at an incredible speed—50 knots has probably been achieved in bursts now.

But the J foil is not for everyone. You've got to be an absolute maestro to control the boat under those conditions. When the boat comes up out of the water and heels to leeward and flies on that foil, they are even able to incline the mast to windward so as to not lose the sail power that most boats are trying to lose when they heel. The real purpose of heeling is to dump excessive wind power out the top of the sail. These things, they don't want to do that—they want to use that energy to drive the thing through the water. That's the J foil.

There's another one they call a T foil, which is the one that I think is more interesting and has a greater commercial future. It's a foil that, if you look at it from behind or coming at you, looks like an upside-down T. It has a vertical dagger board going down into the water that's also shaped like a wing, the section of that thing is shaped like a teardrop—it looks like a table knife sticking down in the water. On the end of the table knife, there's a lateral wing—that's the top of the T (in this case, the bottom of the T because the T is upside down). That foil down there, now, it's well down in the water. It can be fitted with what you might call an aileron, which is a flap on the trailing edge.

That flap can be controlled just like in an airplane so that the T part of the foil on the bottom can develop lift upward or downward. What they're doing with T-foilers now, particularly those designed by Sam Bradfield and his team of genius guys down in Florida, they have devised a trimaran that has three T foils—one in each outer hull and one of them actually on the stern of the main hull, which comprises the rudder, so the vertical knife blade part of that one turns in order to comprise the rudder. Now the boat comes up out of the water, it flies on all three of these T foils. The foil on the downwind side is lifting up the downwind side of the boat and the foil on the stern of the main hull is lifting up the stern of the boat. But the foil on the upwind float, that's down in the water, it's actually pulling downwards, so they can keep the boat dead level even though the wind force is trying to make it heel. So you don't have to incline the mast to windward to keep from spilling wind. Now you've got something you can really control.

I think the future for this type of hydrofoil vessel is really great. There's a tremendous opportunity here to devise wind-powered machines that can also be engine powered, that can go fast, stable, and safe enough, but not a balancing act. So that we can really push out into the future with foil-borne multihulls that can become truly commercial, that is they can keep schedule even if there's no wind, they can motor fast enough to keep schedule.

Because of the apparent wind effect, which is something that we can get into, but it's like hanging your head out of the car window—you're going down the road in calm, but you've got 50 knots of wind blowing over your face. When a sailboat gets going that fast, it generates a lot of its own wind. That's why they can sail faster than the true wind is blowing. I think that particular concept, the apparent wind phenomenon, can be utilized in order to develop sailing vessels in the future that are very much like modern jet aircraft. They will require enormous bursts of power to get them up on foil—if the wind isn't blowing hard, they're really going to have to hit the throttle to get the boat up on foil—but after it's going, now it's generating enough of its own wind so they can throttle back, maybe even shut down, and sail fast in very little wind, at least on some points of sailing. Now we get the opportunity for, say, an ocean crossing, for example, if you're going to ride an ocean liner over to La Havre like they used to. They know so much more about weather systems, and the control of the vessel can be computerized, optimized. I really think we're looking at multihulls that are really going to speak to the energy future of humankind. They'll be a good example, not the only example, but a darn good example of how you can apply modern technology to an ancient concept and thereby find a way ahead for this really rather alarming predicament that humanity finds itself in today. Did I answer that question?

Robin: Oh, yes, you did. My mind's racing a million miles here with this one.

Jim: It's a lot of fun to talk about this stuff. What we really need to do, we're going to try to do it on our site, I think, is get a few people, not just one dude like me who's a blah-blah, but get a few people to present alternative or augmenting views in a conversation like this. But we're going to have to shorten it down, ay? (laughter)

Robin: **I know you have a new website. Can you just tell us a little bit about it?**

Jim: It has come about as a result of my interest in modern multihull history. Because I was around a bit in the early days, I know that there are thousands of stories that are just like mine out there that are dying to be told. So, we've made a website where we can all do the telling. We're asking for submissions from the public—to send us whatever it is they want to say that's multihull related, particularly how multihulls have shaped their lives, and we're getting some neat stuff on there. We've just gotten started.

I've neglected the site in the last few weeks because I'm trying to get a book out. I guess I should tell you about that too. I've been working on a book for years. We're going to publish it on demand and online. It talks about many of the things that I've tried to address today.

The website is www.OutRig.org and everything is free on OutRig, but we have a commercial counterpart which is outrigmedia.com. We're hoping to gather some of this historical information, put it together as information products, and make it widely available.

Robin: That sounds very good.

Jim: So much of the stuff we've been talking about has been objective—comparing this with that; why you want this kind of boat instead of that kind of a boat—all of those are objective considerations. Whereas when it comes right down to it, Robin, the reason a guy or a gal chooses a boat or a boat type is not objective. It's very subjective. No matter what I say or what anybody else says, what you want is the kind of a boat that turns you on, that you can learn to love; something that will grab you right by the pit of the pituitary and say, "Yes, you can love me." If you can find a boat like that, you're going to love and hate it either way, like it is with all things, and yet, if you really love it, you're going to be able to contend with its shortcomings and be able to really enjoy its advantages. All of this stuff about monohull, multihull, catamaran, trimaran, proa, and so on, what you're really looking for in there is something that is just so darn fascinating to you that it lights the fire in your belly and you can run with it.

Closing

Robin: Jim, I want to thank you for being so generous with your time today. It's been fascinating. You've certainly piqued my curiosity about multihulls and even convinced me to try a trimaran, and I'm on a monohull.

Jim: You ought to try one, but it may ruin your life.

Robin: It can't be any worse. I look forward to seeing your new website and reading your book.

Jim: Thank you very much for providing a format where I was able to really shoot my mouth off, if it means something.

Robin: We've all been listening with baited breath.

Jim: I'd be glad to hear what people think. They can write to me—my email address is OutRig.org@gmail.com and my website is OutRig.org.

Key Points

- The real difference between multihulls and monohulls is people; people willing to embrace the multihull concept are really embracing a different attitude toward the sea.

- One disadvantage of a multihull is limited load carrying capacity. Consider what you're going to take with you. You sometimes have to decide whether to go against the wind or bear off in order to reduce the pounding, which is particularly bad in big catamarans.

- A trimaran has one large central hull and two smaller outer or outrigger hulls. A trimaran can run fine on one engine. There is a place on a trimaran bow to attach the head or jib stay.

- A catamaran doesn't have a bow. It usually has twin rudders and you have to hook them together. A catamaran's stirring linkages are complex and expensive. The catamaran has two centerboards/trunks; a trimaran has only one.

- A catamaran's widely spaced hulls can straddle a wave crest. A trimaran's float, or outer hull, is not as far from the main hull as the two catamaran hulls are from each other, so there's less room to straddle in a trimaran.

- The catamaran has to drag its two hulls through the tack. A trimaran, properly designed, only has to drag one hull through the tack. For that reason, trimarans are more maneuverable than catamarans. It's easier to tack them.

- Trimarans are better upwind—they communicate with the pilot in a more direct manner. A trimaran will tell you in no uncertain terms that you're driving the daylights out of your boat because the lee floats, the bow of the downwind outrigger, will go right through the crest. That's normal behavior when driving the boat hard to windward.

41

- Trimarans are safer than catamarans. They are less likely to capsize, and, if they do, trimarans are habitable when capsized and catamarans are not. When a trimaran capsizes, its outer hulls form giant airlocks that hold the main hull up high enough to make it habitable even when the boat is upside down. You can cut a hole in the hull or open the safety hatch in a capsized trimaran to get oxygen inside the main hull while the vessel is capsized.

- A proa has one main hull and only one smaller outrigger hull on one side of the boat, usually to windward.

- Hydrofoils are racing trimarans fitted with J, T, and/or ladder foils; hydrofoils are underwater wings that accomplish the same thing in water that airplane wings do in air.

Other Books

If you enjoyed this book, then you'll love...

Buying a Boat, Captain Chris Kourtakis

Marine Surveys, Rob Scanlan

Insuring a Boat, Mike Smith

Financing a Boat Purchase, Jim Coburn

Rent Your Boat, Brian Stefka

Search and Rescue, Alan Sorum

Bad Storms/Heavy Weather, Timothy Wyand

Digital Selective Calling (DSC), the Automatic Identification System (AIS), and Automated Radio Checks (ARC), Captain Chris Kourtakis

Multihulls, Jim Brown

Custom Electrical Panels and Wiring Harnesses, Mark Rogers

Making a Living as a Professional Sailor, Brian Hancock

Seven Tips for a Successful Sale of Your Used Boat, Robin G. Coles

4 Essential Steps to Buying Your Boat

Boating Secrets: 127 Top Tips to Help You Buy and/or Enjoy Your Boat, print copy (8.5" x 11", 230 pages)

Or, go to: Boating Secrets Website (BoatingSecrets127TopTips.com) for all our books, audios, and transcripts

Acknowledgements

Life is full of challenges. Believe me when I say I've had more than my share. But I truly believe that everything happens for a reason – good or bad. Not that one necessarily asks for the bad things to happen.

Only after having my life turned upside down – starting in June 2000, when I was misdiagnosed with Ms, and then learning, a year later, that I had cancer and wasn't likely to live ten more years – did I decide it was time to live life and not sweat the small stuff so much like I used to. So here I am writing this acknowledgement and the first two people I'd like to thank are my doctors, Dr. Michael Britt and Dr. Kenneth Miller, for keeping me healthy. It wasn't easy.

This decision took me to learn to sail, travel Europe more, and visit over 300 marinas in the US and abroad. It was an assignment gone wrong that turned out TheNauticalLifestyle.com and this book. But I'm glad I was given that opportunity. Thank you to everyone I've met and spoken with in the marine industry, you have all widened my horizons in one way or another.

To Jim Brown it seems like only yesterday we were juggling our schedules to do this interview. Your willingness to give of your time and knowledge for this project is truly appreciated and I thank you from the bottom of my heart. I wish you much success.

Others I'd like to thank are Fifi Ball and Marjory Thomas, my writing buddies for five plus years. Their encouragement and tweaking of my articles really helped. Especially Fifi for taking the recording transcripts and turning them into a readable work. And Mark Hendricks, his countless hours of phone support as this project took on a life of its own.

I would be remiss if I didn't mention my aunt, Dorie Shoer, and my boys Joshua and Lincoln Sziranko, who would throw my words, "Go for it" back at me when I talked about this project. Last but not least, thanks to my best friend George Ryder for encouraging me to follow my dreams and opening up my world. I love you guys!

About the Author

Robin G. Coles is a passionate marine enthusiast and sailor who has interviewed countless industry experts as well as visited, interviewed personnel at, written about, and photographed hundreds of marine ports in the US and abroad.

The ocean both scares and exhilarates her, as it should any boater – one minute it is as calm and smooth as glass; the next a stark raving maniac, as crazy as life itself.

Though Robin has had many challenges in her life, she has always managed to bounce back. Her time on the ocean has been her most rewarding.

Robin has authored a newspaper column and a variety of articles, newsletters, case studies, reports, and technical documents about boating and non-boating topics.

Robin has been a shutterbug from as far back as she can remember. Her photographs have been featured on the cover of the 2008 Winthrop Phonebook, at the 2009 IPEVO show in Las Vegas, and on a local real estate website. To see/read her boating related media, go to TheNauticalLifestyle.com/TransientTalk. Her non-boating related media can be found at RGColesAndCo.com. Photography can be found at NauticalLife.SmugMug.com.

In Robin's spare time she loves to walk the beach, photograph a variety of subjects, read good detective stories, travel, cook, crochet hats for preemie babies and shawls for four-to-six year olds in cancer wards, write, and sail Boston Harbor.

Robin lives on a peninsula near Boston Harbor and Logan Airport, where she sails and works with business owners around the world via satellite phone and internet.

Contact Information

Robin G. Coles
P O Box 520461
Winthrop, MA 02152

339-532-8334

robin@TheNauticalLifestyle.com

Facebook: www.facebook.com/TheNauticalLifestyle

Twitter: www.twitter.com/NauticalLife

Website: www.TheNauticalLifestyle.com

Blog: www.TheNauticalLifestyle.com/TransientTalk

Photographs: www.NauticalLife.SmugMug.com

Non-boating related articles/website: www.RGColesAndCo.com

Pinterest: www.pinterest.com/rgcoles

YouTube: youtube.com/user/colesrg

Linkedin: www.Linedin.com/in/RobinGColes

www.ingramcontent.com/pod-product-compliance
Lightning Source LLC
LaVergne TN
LVHW021547080426
835509LV00019B/2877